Amazing Animals

Sharks

Skip Counting

Saskia Lacey

Consultant

Lorrie McConnell, M.A.
Professional Development Specialist TK–12
Moreno Valley USD, CA

Publishing Credits

Rachelle Cracchiolo, M.S.Ed., *Publisher*
Conni Medina, M.A.Ed., *Managing Editor*
Dona Herweck Rice, *Series Developer*
Emily R. Smith, M.A.Ed., *Series Developer*
Diana Kenney, M.A.Ed., NBCT, *Project Manager*
June Kikuchi, *Content Director*
Stacy Monsman, M.A., *Editor*
Michelle Jovin, M.A., *Assistant Editor*
Fabiola Sepulveda, *Graphic Designer*

Image Credits: front cover, p.1 Martin Strmiska/Alamy; p.10 Charles Hood/Alamy; p.11 Jeff Rotman/Alamy; p.12 Martin Strmiska / Alamy Stock Photo; p.13 Stocktrek Images/Alamy; p.14 AMNH/J. Sparks, D. Gruber, and V. Pieribone supplied by Wenn/Newscom; p.15 Andy Murch/VWPics/Newscom; p.16 Kelvin Aitken/VWPics/Alamy Stock Photo; p.17 Gary Doak/Alamy; pp.18, 19 Paulo de Oliveira/NHPA/Photoshot/Newscom; p.19 (bottom right) Timothy J. Bradley; pp.26, 27 Aji Styawan/NurPhoto/Sipa USA/Newscom; all other images from iStock and/or Shutterstock.

Library of Congress Cataloging-in-Publication Data

Names: Lacey, Saskia, author.
Title: Sharks / Saskia Lacey.
Description: Huntington Beach, CA : Teacher Created Materials, [2018] |
    Series: Amazing animals | Audience: K to grade 3. | Includes index. |
    Identifiers: LCCN 2017049048 (print) | LCCN 2017061089 (ebook) | ISBN
    9781480759930 (eBook) | ISBN 9781425857431 (pbk.)
Subjects: LCSH: Sharks--Juvenile literature. | Sharks--Conservation--Juvenile
    literature.
Classification: LCC QL638.9 (ebook) | LCC QL638.9 .L324 2018 (print) | DDC
    597.3--dc23
LC record available at https://lccn.loc.gov/2017049048

Teacher Created Materials
5301 Oceanus Drive
Huntington Beach, CA 92649-1030
http://www.tcmpub.com

ISBN 978-1-4258-5743-1

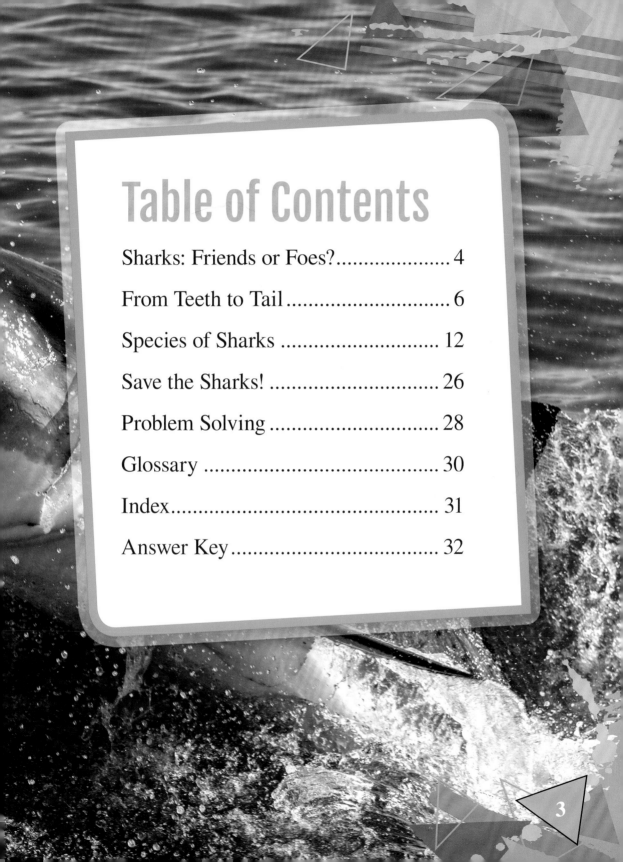

Table of Contents

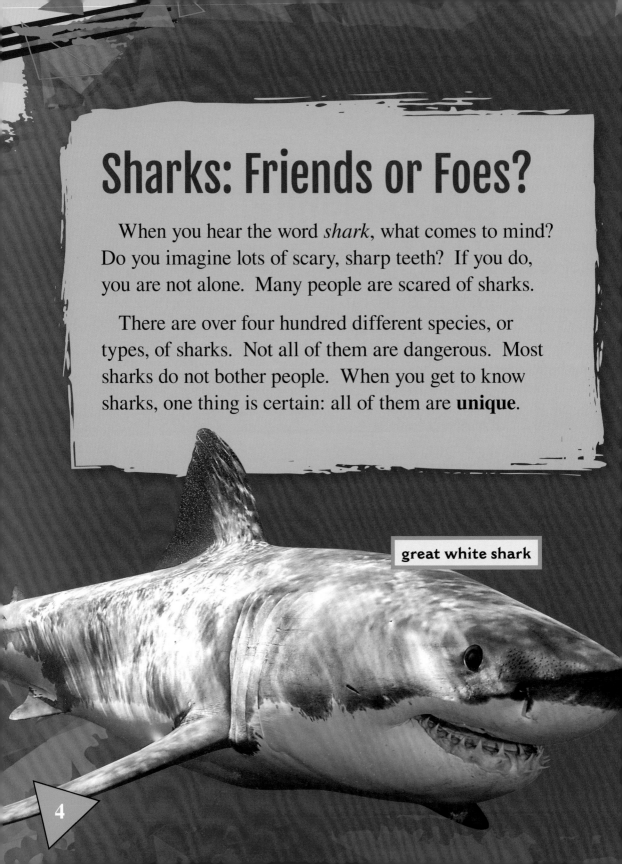

Sharks: Friends or Foes?

When you hear the word *shark*, what comes to mind? Do you imagine lots of scary, sharp teeth? If you do, you are not alone. Many people are scared of sharks.

There are over four hundred different species, or types, of sharks. Not all of them are dangerous. Most sharks do not bother people. When you get to know sharks, one thing is certain: all of them are **unique**.

great white shark

Imagine your class visits an aquarium during a school field trip.

1. So far, your friends have counted 37 tanks. They ask you to keep counting at an exhibit with 4 tanks. What are the next four numbers after 37?

2. Aquarium workers are feeding food pellets to fish. As they toss food pellets into the tank, they count back to keep track of how many food pellets are left. Right now, there are 122 food pellets. When counting back from 122, what are the first four numbers they will say?

reef shark

From Teeth to Tail

With so many species of sharks, there is a lot of variety in what they look like. But, many sharks share the same **anatomy**.

All sharks are fish. This means that they use **gills** to breathe and **fins** to swim. Caudal (KAWD-uhl) fins, or tail fins, give sharks strength. As sharks move from side to side, their fins push them through the water.

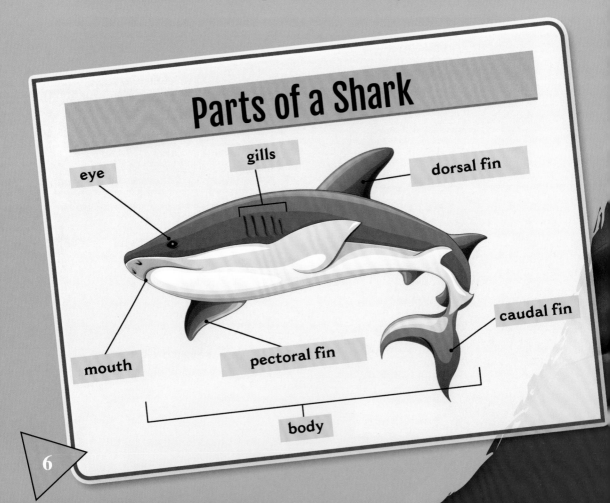

Parts of a Shark

- eye
- gills
- dorsal fin
- mouth
- pectoral fin
- caudal fin
- body

While at the aquarium, Toby notices that some sharks have 5 gills on each side of their bodies.

1. Skip count by 5s to prove how many total gills one shark has.

2. There are 4 sharks in the tank. Draw a number line similar to the one below. Choose a number to skip count by, and use the number line to prove how many gills four sharks have.

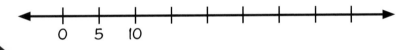

0   5   10

Reef sharks use their strong fins to make quick turns.

Most sharks have pointed fins and **snouts**. Blue sharks and great white sharks have this shape. It helps them cut through water and swim quickly. Some of these sharks can swim over 40 miles per hour (64 kilometers per hour) when they chase **prey**.

Other species, such as the whale shark and the angel shark, have flat, round snouts. Sharks use this type of snout to bury themselves in the sand. Then, they hide as they wait for prey to swim by.

whale shark

blue shark

9

Sharks are known for their grins. Unlike humans, sharks have rows and rows of teeth. When a shark loses a tooth, a tooth from another row moves forward to replace it.

Some sharks have very sharp teeth that help them tear apart food. Others have flat teeth that help them crush shells to eat what is inside. Sharks have the teeth they need to hunt prey that live in their **habitats**.

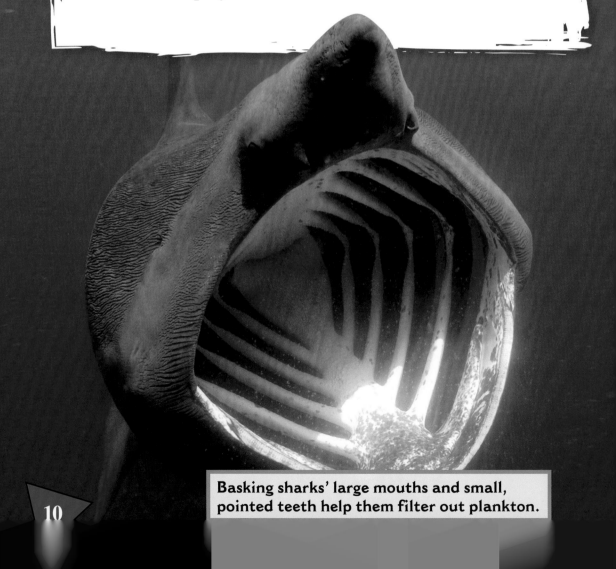

Basking sharks' large mouths and small, pointed teeth help them filter out plankton.

The gift shop at the aquarium sells bags of plastic shark teeth.

1. Each bag holds 10 plastic teeth. Tara buys 8 bags. Use the blanks to skip count by 10s to prove how many total teeth Tara buys.

   10, ___, ___, ___, ___, ___, ___, ___

2. What patterns do you notice when skip counting by 10s?

Sand tiger sharks use their sharp teeth to eat small bony fish.

Species of Sharks

All sharks share some **traits**, such as gills and fins. However, there are other things that make each species unique.

Whale Sharks

The biggest fish in the world is the whale shark. Whale sharks can be up to 59 feet (18 meters) long. That is longer than a school bus! They hunt by swimming with their mouths open. As they swim, they catch tiny prey and plants. Water flows through their gills while food stays in their mouths.

Two scuba divers swim alongside a whale shark.

This whale shark gets a mouthful of water and food.

LET'S EXPLORE MATH

While at the aquarium, the class learns that the 100 peso bill from the Philippines has whale sharks on the back.

1. Students see a display of seven 100 peso bills. Use the blanks to skip count by 100s to prove how many total pesos the money is worth.

   100, ____, ____, ____, ____, ____, ____

2. What patterns do you notice when skip counting by 100s?

Chain catsharks see each other as having bright green skin.

Chain Catsharks

Whale sharks are named for their size, while chain catsharks are named for their skin. Their name comes from the chain pattern on their brown-and-yellow skin.

Chain catsharks are deep-water fish. They hunt squid, fish, and worms. Chain catsharks live on the ocean floor. Their skin helps them blend in with the sand. But catsharks can easily see each other. They see other catsharks as glowing green shapes.

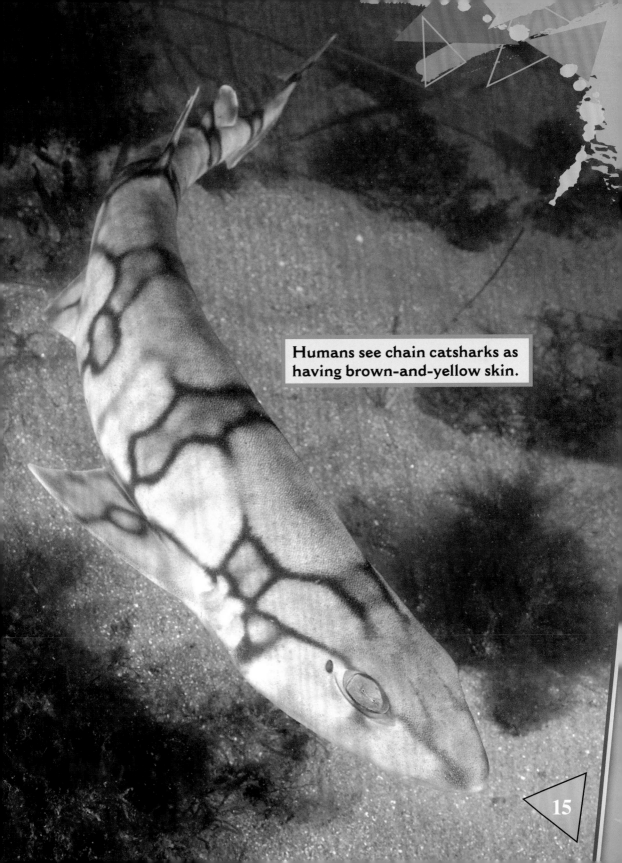

Humans see chain catsharks as having brown-and-yellow skin.

angel shark

Angel Sharks

Like catsharks, angel sharks live on the sea floor. When angel sharks hunt, they first hide in the sand. They wiggle back and forth until their bodies are covered. Only their eyes can be seen. Then, they wait for prey to pass. Angel sharks can lay still on the sea floor for over a week! When angel sharks see prey, they pop out of the sand and snap their jaws shut.

A scuba diver swims by a covered angel shark.

Goblin Sharks

Goblin sharks also live on the sea floor. These pink sharks are known for their unique jaws. When they hunt, they can stretch their jaws out of their mouths by up to 3 inches (8 centimeters)! They can do this because their jaws are not attached to their mouths. Instead, they are connected to flaps of skin. The skin unfolds to let the shark catch prey. This trait lets them catch prey from farther away.

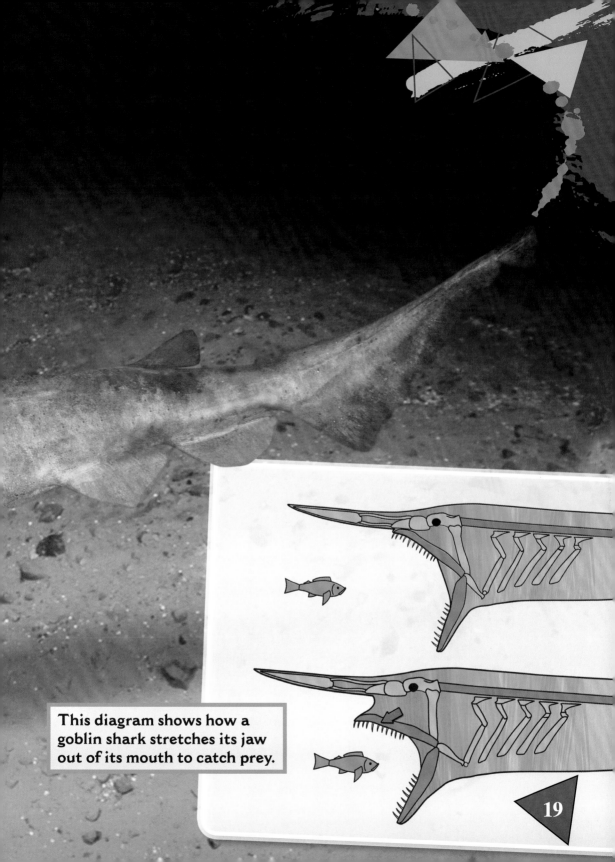

This diagram shows how a goblin shark stretches its jaw out of its mouth to catch prey.

Nurse Sharks

In warm, **shallow** waters, people may spot nurse sharks. Their brown color helps them to blend in with the sand. These sharks move slowly and eat small creatures. The strong jaws and size of nurse sharks scare some people. After all, they can be up to 14 ft. (4 m) long! But nurse sharks are gentle. They will not attack humans unless they feel they are in danger.

A diver swims by a nurse shark.

The two pointed objects near nurse sharks' mouths are actually part of their noses.

hammerhead shark

Hammerhead Sharks

Hammerhead sharks stay near the water's surface. These sharks are easy to spot by their unique heads. Their huge size makes them stand out, too. Some can weigh up to 1,000 pounds (450 kilograms)!

As they swim, these sharks swing their heads from side to side. This lets them use their wide-set eyes to see all around. They can see both in front of and behind themselves as they swim. This trait helps hammerhead sharks hunt and stay safe.

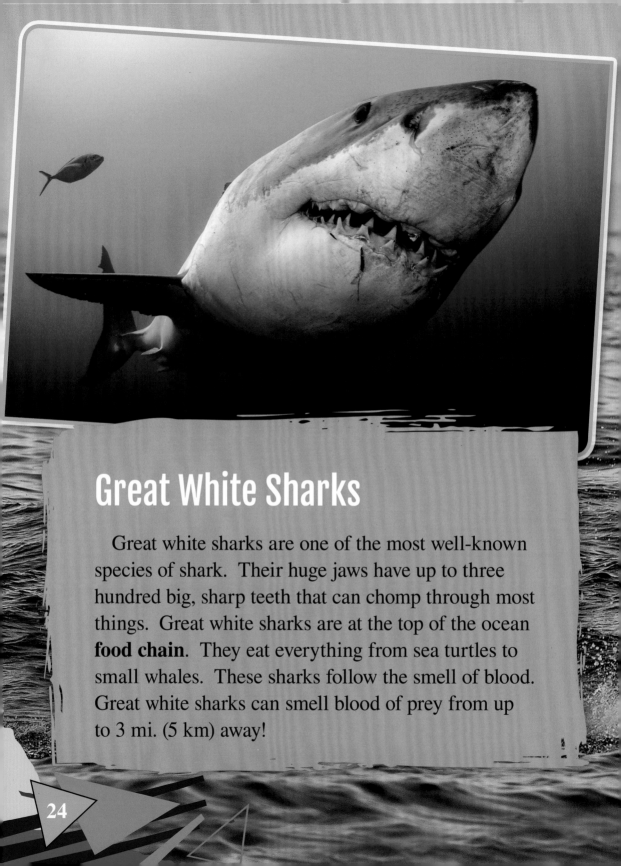

Great White Sharks

Great white sharks are one of the most well-known species of shark. Their huge jaws have up to three hundred big, sharp teeth that can chomp through most things. Great white sharks are at the top of the ocean **food chain**. They eat everything from sea turtles to small whales. These sharks follow the smell of blood. Great white sharks can smell blood of prey from up to 3 mi. (5 km) away!

Great white sharks' teeth have tiny, saw-like edges.

A great white shark jumps out of the water to catch a seal.

Save the Sharks!

Humans hunt sharks for food and sport. This is not good for sea life. Sharks help keep the food chain in balance. People need to work together to keep sharks safe. Keeping the oceans clean can keep sharks safe. Not buying products with shark in them, such as food and clothing made from sharks' meat and skin, can help, too.

Sharks come in all shapes and sizes. Some sharks are dangerous and some are harmless. But each is a unique creature that needs to be protected.

⚙️ Problem Solving

Tiger sharks can swim up to 20 miles per hour. With that quick speed, they can travel long distances in short amounts of time. Imagine that scientists track some tiger sharks with electronic tags. Using data from the tags, they find out how far the sharks swim each month.

The table shows how far four tiger sharks swam from January to June. Use skip counting to find the pattern for each shark's swimming habits, and complete the table. Then, describe each shark's swimming pattern.

Shark Name	January	February	March	April	May	June
Pete	10 mi.		20 mi.	25 mi.		35 mi.
Jet	25 mi.	35 mi.			65 mi.	
Walt	47 mi.		67 mi.	77 mi.		97 mi.
Sparkle	102 mi.		302 mi.		502 mi.	

Glossary

anatomy—the parts that make up a living thing

fins—flat, thin parts that stick out from the bodies of fishes and help them swim

food chain—a series where one type of living thing is food for another type of living thing

gills—parts of fishes' bodies that are used for breathing

habitats—places where things live

prey—living things that are hunted by other living things for food

shallow—not deep

snouts—long noses of some animals

traits—features that make people or things different from others

unique—unlike anything else

Index

SHARK SIGHTED TODAY

ENTER WATER AT OWN RISK

Answer Key

Let's Explore Math

page 5:

1. 38, 39, 40, 41
2. 121, 120, 119, 118

page 7:

1. 5, 10; 10 gills
2. Number lines will vary but should show that four sharks will have a total of 40 gills.

page 11:

1. 10, <u>20</u>, <u>30</u>, <u>40</u>, <u>50</u>, <u>60</u>, <u>70</u>, <u>80</u>; Tara buys 80 teeth.
2. Answers will vary but may include that every number has a 0 in the ones place or that every number increases by 1 in the tens place.

page 13:

1. 100, <u>200</u>, <u>300</u>, <u>400</u>, <u>500</u>, <u>600</u>, <u>700</u>; The money is worth 700 pesos.
2. Answers will vary but may include that every number has a 0 in the ones place and in the tens place or that every number increases by 1 in the hundreds place.

Problem Solving

Pete—February: 15 mi., May: 30 mi.

Jet—March: 45 mi., April: 55 mi., June: 75 mi.

Walt—February: 57 mi., May: 87 mi.

Sparkle—February: 202 mi., April: 402 mi., June: 602 mi.

Descriptions will vary. Example: Pete swam 5 mi. farther each month than the previous month, Jet and Walt swam 10 mi. farther, and Sparkle swam 100 mi. farther.